The Time of Your Life

Other titles in this series

Life in a Sex-Mad Society
by Joyce Huggett

User's Guide to the Media
by David Porter

Dead Sure?
by J. John

Frameworks for Living

The Time of Your Life

Alan MacDonald,
Tony Campolo,
Vance Hays,
Steve Lawhead,
David Neff,
Val Howard,
Bob Bittner,
Robert Kachur

Inter-Varsity Press

Inter-Varsity Press
38 De Montfort Street,
Leicester LE1 7GP,
England

First published 1989

Distributed in Australia by
ANZEA Publishers.
Australian ISBN 0-85892-401-3

British Library Cataloguing in Publication Data

The time of your life.
1. Young persons. Christian life
I. MacDonald, Alan II. Series
248.8'3

ISBN 0-85110-669-2

Set in Baskerville
Photoset in Great Britain by Parker Typesetting Service, Leicester
Design and illustration by Spring Graphics, Saintfield, N. Ireland
Printed in Great Britain by Collins, Glasgow.

Inter-Varsity Press is the book publishing division of the Universities and Colleges Christian Fellowship (formerly the Inter-Varsity Fellowship), a student movement linking Christian Unions in universities and colleges throughout the United Kingdom and the Republic of Ireland, and a member movement of the International Fellowship of Evangelical Students. For information about local and national activities write to UCCF, 38 De Montfort Street, Leicester LE1 7GP.

Contents

"Add together all the small choices we make about our time and you get our lifestyle."

Acknowledgements

Ch. 1 © Universities and Colleges Christian Fellowship 1989. *Ch. 2* Originally published as 'Party Politics: Could I Whoop It Up With Friends Without Compromising My Standards?' by Robert Kachur in HIS magazine, October 1986. Copyright © 1986 Robert Kachur. *Chs. 3 and 5* 'Reading between the lines' and 'The good video guide' © Alan MacDonald 1989. *Ch. 4* Originally published as 'To Drink or Not to Drink: Now That's a Tricky Question' by David Neff with Robert M. Kachur in HIS magazine, April 1982. Copyright © 1982 David Neff. *Ch. 6* Originally published as 'Sunday: This Day's for You' by Vance Hays in HIS magazine, October 1985. Copyright © 1985 Vance Hays. *Ch. 7* Originally published as 'How to Find Gold on the Silver Screen' by Bob Bittner in HIS magazine, March 1985. Copyright © 1985 Bob Bittner. *Ch. 8* Adapted from *Rock of This Age* by Steve Lawhead. Rev. ed. © 1987 by Steve Lawhead; first ed. © 1981 by InterVarsity Christian Fellowship of the USA. *Ch. 9* Originally published in *Ideas for Social Action* by Anthony Campolo (Grand Rapids, Mich.: Zondervan, 1983). Copyright © 1983 Youth Specialities. Used by permission.

Chs. 2, 4, 6, 7 and 8 are used by permission of InterVarsity Press, PO Box 1400, Downers Grove, Illinois 60515, USA.

Introduction

This book is about choices. Not the big choices: 'What career shall I follow?' or 'Shall I get married?' But the smaller choices: 'What friends shall I make?' 'Which film shall I watch?' 'How should I be involved in society?' 'Should I go to this party?'

There are books to help you with the big choices in life, but the smaller ones crop up more often. Every week they need to be made. Add together all the small choices we make about our time and you get our lifestyle.

This is not a 'giving up' book. It does not set out to make you give up drinking, playing sport or going to rock concerts. But it does encourage you to think through your choices. In this respect it is more like an 'adding flavour' book. Its chapters seek to enrich the enjoyment of your time by putting God at the centre of it.

If this is true, our time won't be devoted only to ourselves, and that is why the last chapter is about social action. If Christians are to enjoy society's benefits they should also be the first to fight for a just and caring society to live in.

Not all the choices in this book are simple ones. Neither have we aimed at giving you a foolproof answer to every question you will face. The authors write not only from theological theory but also from their own hard-earned experience. The result, I hope, is a book that clearly points out the direction to take. From there on you're on your own – or rather you're in the company of Jesus.

Alan MacDonald

chapter one

Walking the tightrope by faith

I remember hearing some time ago about a young man who announced to his friends that he was going to look for a job in Christian work. His reason was that he found it difficult to relate to the world. Because he felt more comfortable around Christians, he thought that entering full-time Christian work would solve his problem.

Another young man, however, decided that Christians were all dull and out of touch. 'Catch me getting to be like that,' he said. 'I'm going to mix as much as possible with the world outside and show people how Christians can enjoy themselves.'

Needless to say, both men ran into difficulties. The first became so cocooned by the so-called protection of his Christian surroundings that the few bridges he had with the world

were soon demolished one by one. He also became the kind of person our second example despised. This other young man was, after only a short time, totally integrated into his worldly surroundings. His integration *into* the world soon became influence *within* the world and that influence eventually became no more than action *on* the world's terms. There is now no outward evidence that he is a child of God.

The aliens

I am always amazed that God has placed us in a situation which, in human terms, is so alien, if not positively threatening to our new, reborn lives. And yet it is in this very situation that we learn how to be the people God created us to be. If that were not the case, God would have taken us out of the world the moment we became Christians.

Finding our place in that world, however, with all that this implies, is no easy task. It seems that we swing between two extremes like a pendulum.

Many Christians, for example, are reluctant to have real friendships with people who do not know the Lord. They are afraid to become too involved because they fear the dangers of worldly influence or corruption.

"Afraid . . . fear the dangers . . ."

'What's in it for me?'

There is nothing wrong with a desire to remain untainted by the world's influence. The J. B. Phillips translation of *Romans 12:2* is an excellent warning for every one of us: 'Don't let the world squeeze you into its mould.' Christians could be forgiven for thinking that the best way to achieve this is to escape into their churches and fellowships and keep out of harm's way.

In trying to escape the world's influence, however, we can run the risk of isolating ourselves from it, thereby doing two things: first, removing ourselves from what is perhaps the most effective environment for victory over sin, the victory which ultimately brings glory to God; and second, cutting off a vital channel of witness to a world which God has told us to reach.

I believe too, though, that many try to escape because they simply feel out of place and ill at ease in the world outside. It is all too easy, when feeling this way, to forget that the Christian should be prepared to feel ill at ease – for the sake of the unbeliever. We cannot and should not expect the initiative to come from anyone else but ourselves, both individually and as a church. We must not expect those without Christ to feel at ease in our 'Christian' culture. Society has fallen so far away from the standards and values of Scripture that the average unbeliever has no frame of reference by which he can start to understand Christian truth or behaviour. It is therefore up to *us* to come out of that Christian culture and build the necessary bridges to meet him at his level of need. And we can only do that if we fully understand what makes him tick. That means getting involved on his terms, even if we do sometimes feel uncomfortable or out of place.

The other side

Having said all of that, however, there are also many Christians who actually pride themselves on having an easy relationship with the world. They have lots of friendships with unbelievers and probably wonder why so much fuss is made about the subject.

The risk attached to this side of the problem is that such individuals can simply fall into complacency. Things go so well that the Christian fails to spot the dangers – and dangers there certainly are.

. . . and dangers there certainly are.

It is very easy to fall into the trap of the world's thinking, to take on its value system and its mentality. A consequence of this can be that we begin to measure scriptural truth against the world's mentality, rather than the other way round. Truths which should be the bedrock of our relationship with God become eroded away – first by the infiltration and then by the acceptance of worldly thinking. It is then only a matter of time before the thinking turns in to action.

You need look no further than the level of sexual immorality among Christians today, to see how easily this kind of infiltration of our thinking can manifest itself. The percentage of adultery cases among Christians is rising steadily. Premarital sex is considered by many believers to be 'unavoidable'. Even homosexual practice is now openly accepted by many to be an option for some Christians. I have heard Christians, involved in one or other of these, rationalize their behaviour and give 'good' reasons why their behaviour is right.

Two extremes of a pendulum. The over-cautious and the under-cautious. Somehow the balance seems almost impossible to find.

The tightrope balancing act

In the *Gospel of John, chapter 17*, we find the key. Jesus prays to the Father not that he should 'take them out of the world but that (he should) protect them from the evil one' (*verse 15*). There we see the balance. *In* the world but not *of* the world.

The two young men mentioned at the beginning of this chapter do each have a valid point. One is afraid of the world's corruption, the other is afraid of the Christian's piety. Where they go wrong, however, is that neither is seeking his solution in the Saviour. To walk this kind of tightrope takes much more than human wherewithal. It takes faith. Living faith based on a daily intake of Scripture, in which we find the unchanging promises of God, made available to us through Christ. Jesus' words in *John 17* are equally relevant to both these men, even though they may approach what he said from two different points of view. But their relevance is made manifest through faith.

We need faith to live a life pleasing to God in a corrupt world. But we also need faith to avoid the defensive legalism brought about by fear of that same world and to enjoy the many good things it really does offer.

The pressure is off

We can never totally escape the world's corruption, any more than we can totally integrate into it. The former is impossible because of our human frame. The latter, because we are also temples of God's Holy Spirit. Accepting that should bring us a sense of relief. The pressure is off. We have nothing to prove. Now we can begin to taste the excitement of developing into the people God wanted us to be – by faith.

It is only as we are forced to function in an alien environment that we truly experience the greatness of God for ourselves. The nastiness around us causes us to realize the extent of our own sin and failure. The expression 'Circumstances don't make you, they reveal you' is very true. We begin to see very clearly how utterly dependent we are on God's mercy and forgiveness. But we then begin to taste victory in areas of our lives we perhaps never knew existed. This, in turn, brings glory to God because we are walking by faith. Living in the world becomes an exciting challenge and we even find ourselves looking for more opportunities in which we can trust God and develop our faith. We then become real people, God-made people.

The world will never be reached by aliens; neither will it be reached by 'over-identifiers'. It will be reached most effectively by those who are going through the same struggles the unbeliever is going through, by those who face the same hardship, abuse from colleagues, injustices and the rest. It will be reached by real people, mixing with real people.

"We can begin to taste the excitement of developing into the people God wanted us to be."

Jesus our role model

The perfect example of this is Jesus himself. He

moved freely among those whom many considered to be the dregs of society. He quite deliberately put himself into situations that would cause many a twentieth-century Christian to raise at least one eyebrow. The reason he was able to do this, I believe, is that he remained in close fellowship with the Father. If we are walking closely with God, through regular times in the Word and prayer, then we have nothing to fear from the world. We can trust God to guide us as to our involvement in an unbelieving environment.

Taking hold of the unchanging truths of Scripture and applying them daily to our lives will result in stability. Truths such as these: I am forgiven; God is a righteous judge; he cannot tolerate sin; I am blameless in God's sight; he does want the best for my life; and many more. Here are the black-and-white absolutes of the Bible. As we learn to obey unquestioningly in these areas which are crystal clear, we find that our faith is developed to trust God in those areas which are not so clear. We begin to demonstrate a maturity which not only pleases God but is attractive to others and communicates a living Saviour to a dying world.

Val Howard

"Saviour to a dying world.

chapter two

Good times or compromise?

'Lyle Hall – where the fun never ends.' I looked at that banner welcoming me to my hall of residence and wondered what college social life would be like. I mean, I enjoyed social life at school. I liked being with people and dancing and meeting girls. But was I ready for the real thing?

I'd hardly had a chance to get used to my new campus or even get to know my roommate when freshers' week began. Then, for the next six weeks, it consumed me. I had never taken party-going so seriously. ('Don't dress too yuppy,' one Scouse law student warned me. 'Don't wear a tie. Don't get drunk. And don't *ever* refuse a pint.')

So began my initiation into the campus party scene. I got into a clique where people seemed, well, not too superficial. And I made close friends. During the week we worked hard: at weekends we played hard. Living it up wasn't a moral issue for me. It wasn't an issue at all. Just part of life. If I occasionally drank too much, I could count on one of my friends to walk me back to my room, feed me two aspirin and take off my shoes when I dropped into bed. Life was good.

Then in my second year I moved halls, and my party life accelerated intensely. As an old hand, I felt obliged to go to every party we gave – midsummer parties, freshers' parties in September, Halloween parties in October, firework parties, and on and on. I began to drink, dance and go out with girls more often than ever before.

So began my initiation into the campus party scene.

New perspective

Between my second and third years, a lot happened. My mum died of heart failure, and I went to live for the summer with an aunt and uncle. I felt empty inside and began to question what I was doing with my life. Through the influence of a Christian acquaintance, I started attending a hall fellowship group that autumn and became a Christian halfway through my third year. Suddenly I had a whole new set of friends – Christian friends – who seemed to care about me a lot. My old friends cared too, but most didn't understand my new-found faith. Several who thought I was going off the deep end because of my mother's death even tried to talk me out of it.

Sometimes I felt uneasy around my non-Christian friends: I worried that they'd reject

"I had been sending out signals that I didn't care any more."

me if I stood up for my beliefs. At the same time, I worried that I'd give in when they encouraged me to do things I now believed were wrong, such as drinking too much. So I gravitated toward Christian friends and Christian activities and decided to avoid situations where I was most tempted to go back to my old ways – namely, parties.

As my final year began, my new way of life seemed in place. Until I ran into Laura, an old friend, who startled me with her honesty.

'We never see you any more. Is everything OK?'

'Oh, I'm fine,' I said avoiding any mention of change in my life. 'Just very busy.'

'You should go and see Carol.' Carol, who lived with Laura, had been one of my best friends since the freshers' week.

'Is she OK?' I asked.

'Oh, she's all right,' Laura said. 'Just hurt that you never talk to her any more. You should come and visit the flat.'

My heart sank. That night I went to see Carol and apologized for not making time for her. I began to realize that a certain intimacy I'd once shared with her and other non-Christian friends was fading. By cutting back on my time with my old friends, I had been sending out signals that I didn't care any more.

Keeping in touch

I felt confused. On one hand, becoming a Christian seemed to mean making time in my schedule for new things (building friendships with the Christians I was meeting in my hall fellowship, praying, reading the Bible), as well as leaving behind some old things (like parties where drinking and casual sex were rampant). But the very people I hoped would notice a positive change in my life didn't see a thing, because I wasn't spending enough time with them. So should I make more time for old friends who didn't approve of my new faith? What would happen when our beliefs and values caused conflict? Would I have the strength not to back down?

I didn't know. But I also didn't want to lose my friends. So I began to seek them out again – on the bus each day, over meals and even at parties.

I'd always felt comfortable at parties. As a Christian, though, I knew I couldn't take part in everything that went on there. So right away I set two rules for myself. If I started feeling tempted to lust or gossip or sin in any other way (including affirming others' sin by laughing or smiling at it), I would simply leave. And I would never get drunk.

For a while everything went great. Friends I hadn't seen for ages welcomed me back warmly. I began to build relationships again and talk about what was going on in my life, including my faith. Friday and Saturday nights seemed the best times to show my friends that Christians knew how to have fun too – without hurting themselves or anyone else.

But as autumn term progressed, two struggles surfaced that made me more and more uneasy.

First, I worried about the unintentional messages I might be sending out to my Christian friends. At one party, for instance, I was dancing the night away when I spied Keith, a shy, insecure first-year from my Bible study group, guzzling beer and standing with a rowdy group from his hall. He was obviously compromising his standards in order to fit in. I wanted to go up to him and tell him I accepted him as he was, and that he didn't have to follow the crowd.

But then a thought struck me: *What impression am I giving Keith?* I had a beer in my hand (I had nursed the same one all night), I was jumping up and down on the dance floor, and at one point in the evening my drunk but otherwise wonderful friend Sandra ran up, gave me a big hug and spilled beer all over me. I hadn't done anything wrong, but I wondered what Keith was thinking: *My Bible study leader drinks and hangs around with loose women – it must be OK.*

"I wondered what Keith was thinking."

Also, a Bible verse I'd read nagged at me – the one that said I should 'abstain from all appearance of evil' (*1 Thes. 5:22*, AV). Did my going to a party give silent approval to all that went on there?

Second, I still struggled to keep from slipping back into my old lifestyle.

At my girlfriend's hall Christmas party, I didn't know a soul and felt like an outsider. I half-consciously began drinking more than usual. Before I knew it I was drunk. Not rip-roaring drunk – just merry enough to think I could handle any situation. In a way it felt perfectly natural; in my first three years of college I had gone to lots of parties and got more intoxicated than this.

But it also felt strange. I hadn't been drunk for a long time. Even before the effect wore off I felt guilt welling up. I was wrong to drink too much. I wanted to belong too – but instead of turning to God, or even my girlfriend, with my insecure feelings, I drank until I felt a false surge of confidence, just like during freshers' week back in the old days. Maybe I shouldn't have gone to the party in the first place.

"I needed to know how to conduct myself day by day in the real world."

My Christian friends didn't have many good answers about how I should relate to others on campus. The only advice I received about the party scene was 'Don't go.' But sticking around Christians all the time and avoiding everyone else (or darting into the world for a few hours over the weekend to evangelize) didn't satisfy me. I needed to know how to conduct myself day by day in the real world, especially among those with whom I'd had the chance to build relationships. And for me, that meant learning how to approach the centre of social life – parties – as a Christian.

A more experienced Christian advised me that if I wanted my friends to see a change in me and be influenced to consider faith in Christ themselves, I shouldn't drink. Other than that, he assured me that Christians had always wrestled with how to relate to the world at large and urged me to look at some Bible passages.

Jesus and parties

Though it hadn't occurred to me that the Bible might have something to say about the party scene, I decided to look into it during the next several weeks. One passage in particular bothered me: 'Do not be yoked together with unbelievers. For what do righteousness and wickedness have in common? Or what fellowship can light have with darkness? . . . What does a believer have in common with an unbeliever?' (*2 Corinthians 6:14–16*). I wondered, *Am I 'yoking myself together with unbelievers' by going to parties?* I didn't know.

So I kept flipping through my New Testament, and homed in on how Jesus related to the people of his day. I noticed that he attended a local wedding reception (*John 2*). Not only did he attend, I discovered, but he changed 120 gallons of water into fine wine and had it delivered to the banquet master! Apparently Jesus didn't shy away from social gatherings and celebrations – places where some, the passage implies, drank too much. He even contributed to the party spirit.

. . . to influence rather than be influenced.

However, Jesus' behaviour raised the eyebrows of some of his pious contemporaries, who called him 'a glutton and a drunkard' (*Mathew 11:19; Luke 7:34*). It must have been so radical for a righteous teacher to keep the company Jesus kept that the Pharisees didn't know what to make of him. Yet he knew how to eat and drink and have a good time with sinners without sinning himself. He listened to them, sympathized with them, laughed with them – but consistently sought to influence rather than be influenced by them along the way.

Reflecting on those passages and my own party behaviour, I realized that sometimes my friends, not I, did the influencing. When I didn't feel secure in my faith and desperately wanted my old friends to accept me, I would pretend that nothing had changed in our friendship or in my life. In contrast, Jesus not

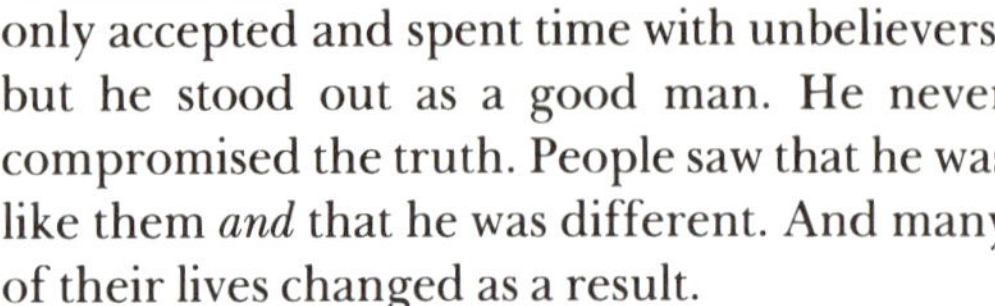

only accepted and spent time with unbelievers, but he stood out as a good man. He never compromised the truth. People saw that he was like them *and* that he was different. And many of their lives changed as a result.

Eventually I became convinced of a few things. Shutting myself off from all the non-Christian friends God had given me wasn't right. I also became confident, as I read through the Bible, that Jesus' command to be 'in the world but not of it' (see *John 17:14–18*) was possible even in the wildest hall. For some Christians who are secure in their faith and feel comfortable in the party scene, parties can be a good place to build friendships – and stand apart.

"A much bigger question than simply, 'Should I go to parties?'"

For other people, I realized, the noise, music and crowds at parties were intimidating, or else offered too many irresistible temptations. But I later learned that many of the friends I had criticized for avoiding parties and discos were busy building bridges with non-Christians in other places – the student union, coffee lounges and inter-hall sports events, to name a few.

From my study of the Bible I also discovered that I was wrestling with a much bigger question than simply, 'Should I go to parties?' I was really asking 'How should I live and act in this world, whether I'm at a party, in my hall, in the cafeteria, out with a girl or anywhere?' To the first question, the Bible says very little: to the second, practical advice abounds.

'Speak truthfully,' the apostle Paul says in *Ephesians 4 and 5*. 'Do not let any unwholesome talk come out of your mouths. . . . Among you there must not be even a hint of sexual immorality, or any kind of impurity, or of greed. Nor should there be obscenity, foolish talk or coarse joking . . . For you were once darkness, but now you are light in the Lord. Live as children of light. . . . Do not get drunk on wine, which leads to debauchery.'

A few words from Peter also helped: 'Do not conform to the evil desires you had when you lived in ignorance. But just as he who called you is holy, so be holy in all you do' (*1 Peter 1:14–15*).

Lessons for a lifetime

As my final year progressed, I still didn't have answers to all my questions about relating to the social scene. And at times I wondered if my struggles were worth it, since my college party-going days were drawing to a close.

But I realized that the past three years had taught me much more than the ethics of party-going. I began to understand – sometimes the hard way – how to interact with people who don't share my most basic beliefs about God and life. I learned not to avoid them or the differences between us for fear of conflict. (Looking back, I would have saved myself some misunderstandings, even with Christian friends like Keith, if I'd talked more openly about my motives and observations.) I discovered personal weaknesses I have to guard against, such as my tendency to rely on alcohol or even other people to bolster my self-confidence. And finally, I learned that my struggle to live in the world without adopting the world's values would not end at graduation; it would continue for the rest of my life.

A few weeks before graduation, my girlfriend Susan and I attended my last hall party. I enjoyed tying up loose ends with friends I had spent time with over the years. As we reminisced and spun circles on the dance floor with our partners, I felt more relaxed than ever.

We talked about where we would be five years from then, why we would and wouldn't miss college, what we would have done differently. And we talked about our differences, even in matters of faith. I was able to explain how my Christian faith had altered my life goals.

Of course the party blared on as we had these conversations, but I didn't feel the need to participate in all that was going on. After

"I was able to explain . . ."

Coke

accepting one drink, I had Diet Pepsi for the rest of the evening. And when a number of couples left early to go skinny-dipping, Susan and I kept dancing.

At one point Geoff, an outspoken student I had known since my first year, approached me.

'You know,' he said, 'when you first got involved with Christianity I thought you had gone off the deep end. I think I even accused you of joining a cult.'

I laughed. 'Yeah, you did, didn't you?'

'Well, I just want to apologize for anything I said or did to make you uncomfortable,' Geoff continued. 'I should have respected your decision. It's obviously not some overnight craze.'

I was overwhelmed. Geoff had never apologized for anything.

'I really appreciate that,' I said. 'It's forgotten.' I paused. 'By the way, if you ever want to talk more about why I take it so seriously . . .'

'Not tonight,' he said. 'Maybe another time.' I smiled as he walked away, thankful that he had seen something more in me than my insecurities. And for tonight, that was enough.

"Geoff had never apologized for anything."

Should I go?

Parties play a big role in today's social life. But party-going means different things to different people. How will you decide where you fit into the party scene? Here are a few suggestions:

Decide ahead of time what kinds of parties you'll attend. Some parties are a good place to catch up with people you might not see otherwise. Others are so wild that no Christian belongs at them: 'For you have spent enough time in the past doing what pagans choose to do – living in debauchery, lust, drunkenness, orgies, carousing and detestable idolatry' (*1 Peter 4:3*). Establishing what's off limits now will make future choices easier.

Be honest. Unless you're consistently open about your lifestyle and convictions as a Christian, people who see you have fun at a party may assume your presence lends a silent seal of approval to everything going on there. Stand firm about who you are.

Be realistic about your weaknesses. Are you prone to drink too much, to flirt, to take drugs? If so, limit your socializing to places where these temptations are reduced.

Be realistic about peer pressure. Peer pressure on campus may be stronger at parties than anywhere else. If you find yourself compromising your beliefs to feel affirmed by others at parties, admit that you're letting others control you – and retreat to safer ground, at least for a while.

Be accountable to your friends. Taking a friend along who knows and shares your beliefs can help keep you honest and clear-headed when you start losing perspective. Agree together that you will each warn the other if you think something's getting out of hand.

Avoid put-downs. If you do decide to go to a party where you can't participate in everything happening, don't be judgmental. Declarations like 'Drinking is a sin' and 'all parties are worldly' only make you sound superior to your friends and reinforce their mistaken idea that Christianity is nothing but dos and don'ts.

Be an influencer. Don't go to parties thinking you're going to change your friends. Ultimately you're not responsible for anyone's actions but your own. Yet your refusal to participate in the excesses of parties may encourage other revellers to have a good time more responsibly.

Robert M. Kachur

What exactly are you supposed to do?

chapter three

Making friends (if you're not good at it)

We've all been there. The party or social where you arrive and find the only people you know haven't turned up. You stand trying to look nonchalant in a corner, clutching a drink which you are sipping too fast and holding a clammy handful of salt 'n' vinegar crisps. Surely someone will rescue you, but it is as if the whole party suddenly gelled into animated groups as soon as you walked through the door. You rehearse opening lines, 'Hello, my name is . . .', 'I

couldn't help overhearing . . .', 'Excuse me, but haven't I seen you waiting for a 38 bus? . . .' It's useless. You just aren't good at making friends.

Many of us can identify with the situation; few of us find it easy. It takes great self-confidence to breeze into a room full of people you don't know and enjoy yourself. Of course, friendships are usually made gradually in situations where we come into contact with people on a regular basis. But what if this doesn't make it any easier? Not everybody finds making friends a natural talent.

People say, 'To have a friend you've got to be a friend.' This is all very well, but how can you be a friend? What exactly are you supposed to do?

Let's put the question differently: What do *I* look for in a friend? What are the qualities *I* would appreciate in a friendship? If we can identify them, then we must ask ourselves if we offer these qualities. You may like to try this exercise for yourself, but here's a personal list:

What makes a friend?

Good company

Most things in life are more enjoyable if shared with someone else. Watching television, playing sport, going to a pub, a concert, the cinema or theatre are all improved by being able to talk about the experience with someone else, providing it's the right kind of person. A good friend recognizes there are two people taking part; he doesn't monopolize the event by giving you a non-stop commentary on how he feels about the film you are watching, neither does he refuse to be drawn on the subject afterwards. He is there to *share* the experience with you. Unless this is a two-way process you might as well do things on your own.

Christians can often appear the opposite of good company. When I was at college I turned down a good number of invitations to the disco or bar because I thought it might 'lead me into sin'. Not surprisingly people soon stopped asking me.

Other Christians accept invitations but make such a point of remaining aloof that their friends feel they are sitting in judgment over them.

Jesus must be the model for our friendships. He was well-known (and criticized) as a friend of tax collectors and sinners. It doesn't follow that he approved of bribery or prostitution because he befriended these people. Yet they must have found him good company to invite him to their houses. Jesus always concentrated on the individuals, not their actions. He must have made them feel their friendship was worth something, whatever their lifestyles.

"Jesus always concentrated on the individuals, not their actions.

Help when needed

Bernard Shaw said of William Archer that he was a friend 'whom I was never sorry to see or unready to talk to'. Archer was the lucky man. When trouble or disaster comes our way what we need is someone who is always ready to listen to us. A real friend is one you can admit your trouble to, knowing that he will immediately drop everything to be with you. Somebody who is always so busy that we have to book a place in his diary a month ahead is not much use. If it is important, a friend will be there.

When I have a problem, advice is not the first thing I need. A good listener is much more valuable. To know somebody else in the world understands how you feel is a great relief and often a friend's great gift is just to keep you company when you are at your lowest.

Even Jesus knew this need. He took his friends to the garden of Gethsemane, not for their advice, but for their company. When he most needed them to be there, they fell asleep. How often is our friendship sleeping just when it's needed?

"A real friend is one you can admit your trouble to."

A sense of humour

Sounds trivial, but what sort of a friendship is it that never laughs together? Laughter can be cruel, but the best kind is an indication that you don't take yourself too seriously. We may choose our friends because of our similarities, but there will always be differences of class, of background, or race, even of the way we keep our room tidy (or not). Friends can recognize the differences and see the funny side to them. If they don't, they will soon fall out.

Being themselves

Sadly, I have known a few people who have tried hard to be my friend – and the more they have tried, the more I've run away. Why does this happen? Because friendships are based on freedom rather than forcing. Someone who is over-eager and over-familiar too soon can have the effect of suffocating a friendship before it starts. We must allow the other person the choice of having us as a friend. If we grasp at their company they will feel pressurized and trapped.

If you are in need of friends this is a hard danger to avoid. Again it's worth asking why Jesus was a good friend. What is clear from the Gospels is that he was always himself. It is impossible to think of a meeting where Jesus puts on some sort of act to impress the other person. Jesus didn't find his value in other people, he didn't need their approval or appreciation. His security was always rooted in the fact that his Father loved him. He didn't get this from friends, but from time alone with God.

"There's almost certainly someone else feeling the same way."

To be ourselves is the stepping-stone to all friendships. People immediately sense a lack of security, someone who is too talkative or too withdrawn. As Christians we must daily drink in that God cares for us like a favourite child, nothing else will stand firm against people's reactions to us.

I look for friends who are good company, who support me, who have a sense of humour and can be themselves. What are you looking for? Ask yourself how much you are willing to *give* these qualities. Are you more concerned with what *you need*? Next time you are among people and feeling lonely, it's worth remembering that there's almost certainly someone else feeling the same way.

Alan MacDonald

chapter four

How much is too much?

There were the inevitable groans when it was announced that all posters advertising Union events could no longer mention alcohol. It wasn't long, however, before a phrase pioneered by one poster caught on: 'The usual beverage will be served.'

That euphemism said it all. As in most places drinking at social events was taken for granted.

Christians have to grapple with alcohol. Take Jane. After becoming a Christian, she decided to make a radical break with the wild lifestyle she and her friends had shared by not drinking. With a few exceptions her friends seemed to respect her decision. Some even wanted to know more about why she had changed, which gave her great opportunities to talk about her faith.

Sharing a sandwich, a pint and his faith . . .

Then there's Eddie, who could often be found at the pub, sharing a sandwich, a pint and his faith with one of his close non-Christian friends over lunch. He had a way of breaking people's preconceived notions that Christianity was simply a list of dos and don'ts and getting them to understand the gospel.

As you can see, Christians take different stands on alcohol. On the way to our decisions, we must explore what the Bible has to say about drinking. For many, the question of whether we as Christians should drink or not boils down to five issues.

Responsibilities

The Bible writers' primary concern about alcohol seems to be that drinking impairs judgment. That's why certain groups of people were asked not to touch it. In the Old Testament, those who served in the worship of God, such as priests, were instructed to avoid drinking when they had spiritual responsibilities: 'You and your sons are not to drink wine or other fermented drink whenever you go into the Tent of Meeting, or you will die. . . . You must distinguish between the holy and the common, between the unclean and the clean; and you must teach the Israelites' (*Leviticus 10:9–11*; see also *Ezekiel 44:21*).

Besides the priests there were the Nazirites, people called to take special vows of obedience and service to God. (You can read about them in *Numbers 6:1–21; Judges 13:2–14; Amos 2:11–12;* and *Luke 1:15*.) Kings, judges and other people in responsibility were advised to abstain, too: 'It is . . . not for kings to drink wine, not for rulers to crave beer: lest they drink and forget what the law decrees, and deprive all the oppressed of their rights' (*Proverbs 31:4–5*). And in the New Testament, when Paul wrote to Timothy and Titus about selecting leaders for the infant church, he told them to choose men 'not indulging in much wine' (*Timothy 3:8*; see also *Titus 1:7*).

So people who claim to serve God must place their God-given responsibilities above their desire for a drink. My responsibilities to help a friend who needed me, to work, whatever – usually seemed less important than those of a king or priest. But, if I drank, would I be up to fulfilling them?

Priorities

With little cash in his pocket (and even less in his bank account), my friend Bob went to buy enough groceries to last until his next wages.

At the checkout counter, he cringed as the assistant rang up the total. He didn't have enough money. She could see it in his face.

All right,' she snapped. 'What don't you want?'

Glancing at the people glowering in line behind him, Bob surveyed his groceries on the counter. The six-pack of Heineken almost shouted at him. He reluctantly pointed to the lager. Crisps and doughnuts were next.

The six-pack of Heineken almost shouted at him.

Fortunately, Bob was able to keep his alcohol and his pocketbook in perspective. Others can't. The Old Testament prophet Joel talks about those who sell children to buy drink (*Joel 3:3*). And Isaiah, taunting those who are heroes at drinking wine and mighty at mixing drinks, is appalled at their lack of concern for the poor (*Isaiah 5:8, 11–12, 20–23*).

You may not be about to sell your firstborn into slavery for a drink. But when finances get tight, you need to decide what will get squeezed out of your budget – booze, or those who need the help you could provide with the money you would otherwise spend on booze?

Health

Hangovers, liver failure, DTs, hallucinations and alcoholism are nothing new. 'Who has needless bruises? Who has bloodshot eyes?' the writer of Proverbs asks. 'Those who linger over wine, who go to sample bowls of mixed wine . . . Your eyes will see strange sights and your mind imagine confusing things' (*Proverbs 23:29–33*). Our bodies are temples of the Holy Spirit. God doesn't want us destroying them with too much drink, food or anything else.

But that's only half the story. The Bible also portrays alcohol in moderation as a good gift from God.

Psalm 104:15 says that one reason God makes the plants grow is so that people may produce 'wine that gladdens the heart of man.' And in *Deuteronomy 14:22–27*, Moses tells the Israelites to honour the Lord by keeping an annual harvest festival, in which a tenth of what is produced – grain, wine, oil, the newborn animals – is to be set aside for a huge feast to be eaten in the Lord's presence. If an individual lived too far from the Israelite worship centre to carry all that produce and meat, he was allowed to convert it into money and buy whatever he wanted to celebrate when he got there. 'Use the silver to buy whatever you like: cattle, sheep, wine or other fermented drink, or anything you wish. Then you and your household shall eat there in the presence of the Lord your God and rejoice' (verse 26).

'I have to tell someone. My wife left me last week.'

Relationships

Some Christians have trouble reconciling a divine command to celebrate with wine and strong drink in the Lord's presence with the picture of God they grew up with. But then Jesus was mistaken for a glutton and a drunkard (*Matthew 11:18–19*) – and that didn't happen by staying away from places where people drank.

Whether Jesus ever drank alcoholic beverages is an irrelevant question; the wine available to him was much less potent than what we have today and was customarily watered down as well. What's important is the company Jesus kept. Jesus got his reputation not because he drank too much, but because he spent time with people who drank too much – people who needed him.

One evening my friend Bob (the one who ran out of money at the supermarket) convinced his mate Steve, a confirmed teetotaller, to have a pint with him at the local to celebrate

his birthday the next day. Steve had always shunned the nearby pubs as a matter of principle, but he reluctantly accompanied Bob to 'The Crown', a crowded, smoked-filled pub.

There they ran into Ashley, a mutual friend. After reminiscing about the good old days, Ashley suddenly became very serious. 'I haven't told anybody this but I think I can tell you,' he said. 'I have to tell someone. My wife left me last week.'

The news jolted them, but they listened as Ashley shared his struggles. After talking a while at the pub, they invited him back to Bob's flat to talk further and pray. Ashley stayed until three in the morning.

After Ashley left, Steve turned to Bob. 'You know, if we hadn't been in that pub, we would never have run into Ashley.'

Most drinkers don't care what you're drinking.

Of course, being with people who drink doesn't give us an excuse for compromising our own principles. But as a rule, most drinkers don't care what you're drinking. (As long as you don't make not drinking the point of your Christian witness, that is. 'I don't drink. I'm a Christian,' lacks the sensitivity Christ had for the people who needed him.) What matters is being with people at their point of need.

Your situation

After reading *Romans 14:21*, I realized that if I decided to drink moderately, I'd have to be careful who I drank with: 'It is good neither to eat meat nor drink wine nor do anything by which your brother stumbles, or is offended, or is made weak' (*New King James Version*).

Even as a light drinker with excellent self-control, I would offend fellow Christians who lack self-control or have a history of alcohol abuse by drinking around them or offering them a drink. That's the kind of offence Paul writes about: causing a person who's weak in a certain area to sin.

But neither Paul nor Jesus worried about offending religious people who were firmly grounded in their beliefs. The question I started asking before I thought about taking a drink with others, then, changed from 'What will these people think?' to 'What do these people need?'

Some of my Christian friends chose not to drink for good reasons. Some couldn't handle alcohol. Others wanted to set a good example in a society where alcohol abuse contributes to a significant percentage of violent crimes, road and industrial accidents, family breakups, debilitating disease and professional incompetence.

A few of my friends, however, chose not to drink for a bad reason: to score brownie points with God. Not drinking can be a practical help to a better relationship with God. But self-righteous teetotalling (or self-righteous anything) never seemed to impress Jesus much.

In the end, only you can decide whether you will drink. Can you do so without impairing your ability to carry out responsibilities, damaging your health, wasting your money or causing someone else to sin? Maybe. But one more piece of biblical advice kept me cautious: 'So, if you think you are standing firm, be careful that you don't fall!' (*1 Corinthians 10:12*).

David Neff with Robert M. Kachur

. . . not to drink: to score brownie points with God.

The Law

Under 16 You cannot be sold or delivered alcohol.

16–18 You can drink alcohol with a meal but not in a public bar.

18 and over You can buy and consume alcohol.

Should my time have been spent on better things?

chapter five

Sport for all?

We sat around the table in the dingy Belgian bar. My brother was fifteen, I was twelve. I'd noticed that our team-mates were beginning to talk rather too loudly and giggle, although nobody had made a joke. Andy, our goal-keeper, ordered his fifth vodka and lime. After all, we had won the tournament. The cup stood proudly in the middle.

'What'll you have?' he asked, leaning unsteadily towards us.

'Two lemonades, thanks,' replied my brother.

Our glasses were filled. Nobody sniggered or made mocking comments; they knew our reasons for being teetotal. We were going to be professional footballers when we grew up.

Sport is a subject that inspires fanatical devotion in some and loathing in others. I ought to declare my interest at the start; I was spoonfed on sport from an early age. Practice over the park every day after school and then three football matches a weekend. Church was fitted in as an unavoidable interruption to the serious business of kicking a ball. Of course, I never did become a professional. No doubt the game was robbed of a great talent, but were all those hours wasted? Should my time have been spent on better things?

Why do we play sport?

Sport seems to have been around as long as man. Mediaeval football matches involved whole village populations; falconry was popular with the Normans; it would hardly be surprising to discover early man was fond of pterodactyl racing.

Why we do it seems to be asking the obvious.

BS
GIVE

There are certain things we get out of it. We want to keep fit, we need recreation, we may value the social side of sport or perhaps we just like to compete. All or some of these things motivate us. Let's consider them individually.

Colour magazines burst with pictures of slim, tanned women and muscle-toned men.

Fitness

Personal fitness has become the boom industry of our age. The parks are full of joggers, our towns boast leisure centres, and colour magazines burst with pictures of slim, tanned women and muscle-toned men. It is easy to be swallowed up in the mindless pursuit of fitness or to dismiss the whole thing as a passing craze. Where should the Christian stand?

The New Testament neither condemns nor recommends sport, but it does talk about it. Paul uses an athlete as an example of how to live as a Christian: 'Run in such a way as to get the prize. Everyone who competes in the games goes into strict training. They do it to get a crown that will not last; but we do it to get a crown that will last for ever' (*1 Corinthians 9:24–25*).

He is not saying that we should all take up running but that spiritual discipline is just like physical discipline. Both require us to submit ourselves totally to an ultimate aim.

'Physical training is of some value, but godliness has value for all things' (*1 Timothy 4:8*). In other words, training our minds to be like Christ is our number-one priority; but training our bodies to obey us can be putting in good practice. If we are physically fit and tuned up then we may find it easier to train the flabby areas of our Christian faith.

Anyone who wants to be an athlete accepts the training as part of the job. This is true of being a Christian. If we rid ourselves of the idea that discipline is a negative thing it may help us to develop healthy patterns in our living for God.

Of course we can't assume this automatically happens. The sad truth is that we often mistake the oyster for the pearl: our bodies become our first priority. (See 'Body worship'.)

Recreation

Why do children play? It is not as if we teach them to do it. From the first, playing is as natural an instinct as breathing and feeding. If we give them a ball they get endless entertainment from rolling and kicking it.

As we grow older the play instinct gets crowded out. The importance of 'getting on in life' is impressed on us. Recreation takes a poor second place or may even be squeezed out entirely as too trivial.

Yet the word itself is important – '*re-creation*'. We have been made with an instinct to refresh, renew and relax ourselves through other activities than work (*Exodus 34:21*). Even in the pattern of the week our Maker has laid down that one day be different from the others. The idea that recreation is less worthy than work or 'spiritual activities' often persists in Christians. But without it we are missing something. 'All work and no play' not only makes Jack a dull boy, but may mean he burns himself out. Recreation is there to recharge our batteries.

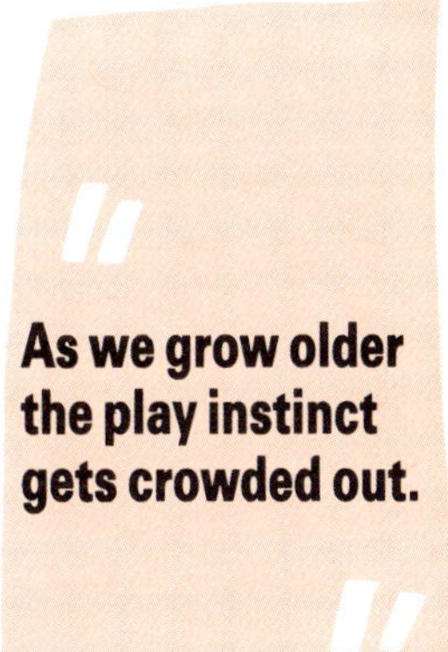
As we grow older the play instinct gets crowded out.

Sport for sociability

Some sports are played solo, but the vast majority are played with other people. There are good reasons for Christians to be involved with everyone else. Jesus talked of us as salt which acts as a preservative to every part of life; without it there is decay (*Matthew 5:13*).

When I play alongside people I get closer to them as individuals. In a team I have to trust them, support them, receive from them and accept the results of their mistakes. It is not so different from Paul's description of the church as a body with many parts. In a sports team and in the church there is a learning process of doing what you are best at and letting others fully develop their talents. There is nothing more frustrating than playing alongside someone who hogs the ball.

Joining a rugby team, tennis club or squash club can be a great way of making friendships. People who have puffed and sweated with you on a pitch are more likely to be open with you in conversation afterwards. This doesn't mean that a Christian plays sport merely to buttonhole his team-mate with the gospel after a match; but it is worth remembering that even in the dressing-room you are Christ's representative.

Body worship

Next time you watch *Dallas* or *Dynasty* count how many overweight people appear in the programme. Or how many do not sport a sun tan?

How many television personalities (not counting comedians) can you think of who have bodies that are obviously out of condition?

The late twentieth century is the age of body worship. The answers to the above questions should show you that looks are what count today. Of course, most of us don't worry too much about our appearance . . . or do we? Try answering some of the questions below honestly.

Stereotypes Do you ever compare yourself with magazine models or television stars? Is there anyone you secretly model yourself on? Are there any features of your face or body that you would really like to change? How satisfied are you with your appearance?

Slimming can be a necessary and healthy discipline, but beware of it becoming obsessive. How much money do you spend on slimming aids, magazines and diets? Does guilt play a big part in your dieting? How much do you think people's reactions to you are affected by your being overweight? Is your self-image accurate or purely subjective?

Body-building If you are into weight training the

Michelle was new to the area and feeling lonely. She had found a church but there was hardly anyone of her own age. One girl at work, Carol, was friendly to her but there was never much time to talk. On top of the loneliness Michelle began to feel guilty that she hadn't told anyone she was a Christian.

Finally, in desperation, Michelle cut out an advert to join a badminton club. She'd never played before in her life. After several weeks of swiping thin air she started to enjoy the game and one night asked Carol if she'd like to play.

After several weeks of swiping thin air she started to enjoy the game.

benefits are numerous: an increase in health, fitness, stamina and strength. The pressure to let body-building dominate your life can be real, however. Is your training routine and diet something you can break when necessary? Is personal vanity motivating you? Are you tempted to use steroids to improve your physique?

Sunbathing For white Northern Europeans, there is nothing like coming back from your holiday with a brown skin to turn your friends green. But does this ever get out of hand? How many hours of our holiday are devoted to sun worship? Do all other things have to take second place to it? Are you spending large amounts on sun-ray sessions and lotions?

The body-temple Bodies in the Bible are described as temples, houses for the Holy Spirit to live in. We should treat our bodies with the same respect that Jewish tradition gave to the temple. But Jesus drove out the money-lenders because what goes on *inside* the temple matters most to God. Similarly, having a body like Jane Fonda's is worthless if inside you are eaten up by pride or jealousy. As Paul says, 'flesh and blood cannot inherit the kingdom of God' (*1 Corinthians 15:50*). So whether we are fat, thin, muscular, puny, brown or white, we should be devoted to building an inner life like Christ's.

Alan MacDonald

Now they are firm friends who play once a week and Carol has even agreed to go along to a church service.

It might be said that Michelle could have found a Christian club to join. Playing for a church, CU or fellowship team of course avoids problems like the bad language or alcohol that are part of some sports clubs. But if Michelle had taken this view she might never have discussed her faith with Carol. The salt Jesus spoke of needed to be on the meat to preserve it, not in the salt-cellar where it is safe but useless. This sort of decision needs to be made carefully and prayerfully.

The competitive instinct

This is where many point the finger of accusation at sport. It encourages aggression, competition, winning at all costs. Shouldn't we avoid something that brings out these instincts in us?

Competition is a part of life that we all have to encounter sooner or later (*James 4:1*). Sport is a battleground where we either come to terms with it or let it take over. The question we must ask ourselves is, how do we cope with winning or losing?

"I felled him from behind like a dwarf lumberjack with a pine."

I once played football against a lad twice my size who would shield the ball from me by the annoying tactic of sticking his rear end out. This made it impossible to get round him. After a while my desire to have the ball became so intense that I felled him from behind like a dwarf lumberjack with a pine. My team-mates congratulated me as if I had done something heroic, but I couldn't help feeling it wasn't a sporting gesture.

Most games end with the tradition of shaking hands with our opponent; if secretly we would rather put our hands round his or her neck then it is a sure sign we haven't come to terms with our competitive instincts.

Striving for excellence in any sport is not wrong, and playing to win is an inevitable part of that. But there are two sets of rules to take into consideration, the rules of the game and God's rules.

By entering a game we agree to abide by its rules. There can be no room for Christian sportsmen or women who want to win even if they have to cheat to do it.

God's rules of course go further. They say 'Love your enemy' even when she's beating you 6–0, 6–0 at tennis.

The Bible is full of men and women who had to learn the lesson of defeat: *that God is more interested in our attitude and obedience than our results.*

The crowd who gathered to watch Jesus hang on a cross must have seen a defeated and broken man who had failed in his mission. From God's viewpoint that moment of defeat was his Son's perfect act of obedience which launched the triumph of saving mankind.

Accepting defeat graciously with a smile is one of the hardest and most valuable lessons of sport. It proves that we don't see ourselves at the centre of the universe.

What about when we win? And who can resist the temptation to punch the air and receive the applause of the imaginary crowd? Nobody is saying we shouldn't enjoy winning. A hangdog expression is not compulsory.

The key is that winning or losing doesn't matter that much to us. We should try to compete against the game rather than against our opponents.

When we win, it should not be an opportunity to display our superiority over them. If we do, every victory will inflate our sense of pride a little more until one defeat bursts our ego like a balloon.

Gary Warner writes: 'I don't believe we really get this right unless through Jesus we can negotiate peace with our need to compete.' This doesn't happen overnight, but through prayer, a sense of humour and experiencing defeats.

Gary Warner, *Competition*, Cook.

The competitive instinct surfaces in many areas of our lives; sport provides an opportunity to tame it rather than be driven by it.

Sport for all?

There are of course those who don't want to play sport at all. It isn't that they have a secret desire to do it, or that they've been discouraged (as many have). They just don't like sport. Fine! The 'Sport for all' slogan doesn't mean that people should be dragged kicking and screaming into a leisure centre. Sport should be available for all, but there is no commandment that we should all play it.

If you are someone who finds the competitive instinct too hot to handle, then perhaps your way of making peace with it is to keep out of competitive sports. There is nothing wrong with avoiding what you know is a danger zone for you.

The competitive instinct surfaces in many areas of our lives.

You may prefer sports that can be non-competitive, such as walking, jogging, swimming, fishing or canoeing.

Perhaps sport is of no interest to you whatsoever. Obviously that is your decision, but it may at least be worth checking if you get the benefits of sport through other areas of your life. Fitness? Recreation? Socializing? If we are too busy for any of these perhaps we are just *too busy*. Christians who are out of condition, burnt-out or living in ivory towers are not likely to be good adverts for the kingdom of God.

The bronzed idol

Finally, having made the case for sport, it is crucial that our involvement is kept in its true perspective.

Idols in the Old Testament came in easily recognizable forms. They were usually cast out of gold or bronze and shaped like bulls, demons, gods or goddesses.

> **"When does a possession or hobby become an idol?"**

Twentieth-century idols come in more subtle forms: BMWs, houses, paper with the Queen's head on it, rock and film stars, the one-eyed god of the television and even the sports teams we support or games we play. This may sound extreme to modern ears. After all we don't bow down and pray to these things like the Babylonians did to their gods. When does a possession or hobby become an idol?

Jesus' teaching about money gives us some clues: 'No-one can serve two masters. Either he will hate the one and love the other, or he will devoted to the one and despise the other. You cannot serve both God and Money' (*Matthew 6:24*).

The danger arises when our sport starts to become our passion. It is a short step to our passion becoming our master. We may not recognize it, but our need to play our sport, buy the right equipment, or watch our team, can become so strong that it begins to dominate our lives. When I was playing three football matches in a weekend there was no doubt what was the top priority in my life. We all know stories about bridegrooms who have cut short their wedding to go and watch their team play. We laugh, but hasn't sport become the dominant idol of their lives?

Ask yourself two questions. First, 'How much of the week is devoted to my chosen sport and how does this compare with the time I devote to God?' Secondly, 'How difficult would I find it if God asked me to give up this sport?'

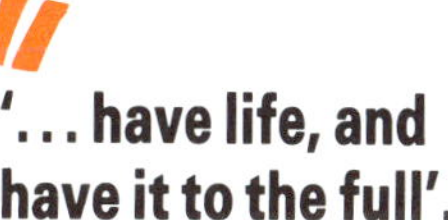

'. . . have life, and have it to the full'.

God's design for living is that we 'may have life, and have it to the full' (*John 10:10*). He made you with the body and talents to enjoy the excitement of sport. What is clear is that nothing should have a higher priority than him in your life. 'You shall have no other gods before me' (*Exodus 23:3*) is the first commandment and one that we often take too lightly.

It is possible to be a keen sportsman or woman and a committed Christian. As George Leonard wrote, 'How we play the game may turn out to be more important than we imagine, for it signifies nothing less than our way of being in the world.'

Alan MacDonald

chapter six

This day is for you

> **Seduced by modern culture we're missing something important: a distinctively biblical rhythm for living.**

What made *Chariots of Fire's* Eric Liddell famous? Of course, he won an Olympic gold medal in the four-hundred metre run. But hundreds of Olympic champions have had their moments and are forgotten. The most important aspect of Liddell's moment of glory wasn't what he did, but what he didn't do – he wouldn't run on Sunday.

Even though most Christians liked the film, I've never heard any express interest in the issue on which Liddell took his stand. Did he believe in something that no longer matters? Should his commitment cause us to re-examine the meaning of Sunday? Perhaps today's Christians have been so seduced by modern culture that they're missing something important – an understanding of how to use time and develop a distinctively biblical rhythm for living.

In the Old Testament, the Sabbath (Friday evening to Saturday evening) was strictly enforced. The fourth commandment says, 'Remember the Sabbath day by keeping it holy. Six days you shall labour and do all your work, but the seventh day is a Sabbath to the Lord your God. On it you shall not do any work, neither you, nor your son or daughter, nor your manservant or maidservant, nor your animals, nor the alien within your gates' (*Exodus 20:8–10*). Sounds narrow-minded, right? Worse than that! The penalty for profaning the Sabbath was death (*Exodus 31:14*). *Numbers 15:32–36* tells about a man who was stoned for gathering firewood on the Sabbath.

On the other hand, the New Testament and

church history suggest a different atmosphere. In Christ there is a new freedom (*Galatians 4:8–11*). So Paul castigates those who make a big deal of Sabbath observance (*Colossians 2:16–17*). And very early in its existence the church ceased observing the seventh day and moved its worship to the first day (although for a time Jewish Christians may well have observed both days).

Why did this happen? Here are two classic reasons people have suggested. First, Jesus was raised from the dead on Sunday. Second, Christians needed to distinguish themselves from Jews, who continued to observe the seventh day.

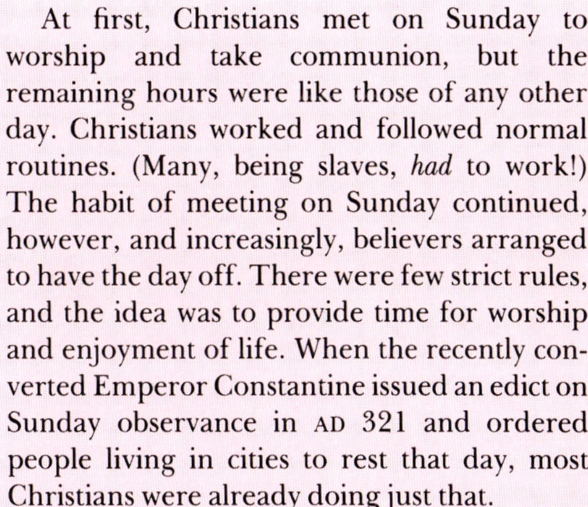

The Sunday habit

At first, Christians met on Sunday to worship and take communion, but the remaining hours were like those of any other day. Christians worked and followed normal routines. (Many, being slaves, *had* to work!) The habit of meeting on Sunday continued, however, and increasingly, believers arranged to have the day off. There were few strict rules, and the idea was to provide time for worship and enjoyment of life. When the recently converted Emperor Constantine issued an edict on Sunday observance in AD 321 and ordered people living in cities to rest that day, most Christians were already doing just that.

It wasn't until the Middle Ages that the Western church moved toward a more formalized Lord's Day. Work and travel were prohibited. The early Reformers generally opposed such an approach, but a strictly observed Sunday was popular among British Puritans, and it has had an effect on our lifestyles even in this century.

Here and now

What should a Christian be doing in the late twentieth century?

The best approach to this issue is to get away from questions about the Sabbath itself and focus more generally on how a Christian

Time is not a resource that belongs partly to you and partly to God.

should use time. The lordship of Jesus is not limited to what people do on Sunday. As his servants, believers are always on call. A Christian can't say to God, 'I belong to you, but my time is my own.' Time is not a resource that belongs partly to you and partly to God. It is all his. And it has been given to Christians as a way to glorify his name.

Now back to the Sunday question. If our time belongs to God, what does he suggest in the Bible about what is appropriate for Sunday?

The Bible establishes two broad principles. First, Christians need to meet together regularly for worship (Hebrews 10:25). The practice of the New Testament church confirms this (Acts 2:42). And so does church practice throughout history. Christian hope always shows a desire to meet with believers. And of course, with few exceptions, Christians worship on Sunday.

Students sometimes ask if their Christian Union or group fellowship is not a good substitute for Sunday services. It's a fair question. The problem is that few of these groups actually function as the church. There is often fellowship, perhaps Bible study and prayer. But there is seldom any connection with other generations of Christians; and there is usually no celebration of the Lord's Supper or baptism, sacraments which Christ commanded the church to administer. Frankly, any good travelling secretary or staff worker in any campus organization will urge you to find and attend a church. That person knows you need to be part of a local congregation. Remember: someday soon you'll leave college, and the only alternative to a local church will be to start one of your own!

Time out

Scripture's second principle is that people need a day of rest. The fourth commandment urges us to cease all work on the Sabbath. And even though Christ fulfills the Sabbath (*Colossians 2:17*), the idea of a day of rest is never rejected in the New Testament. Jesus observed it, although not legalistically like the Pharisees. Our common sense tells us that the Bible is right. Not having regular time off is exhausting. No-one enjoys a nonstop work style. Taking time off is good time management.

Unfortunately, the pressure is on to work all the time. I recently urged a student group not to study on Sunday, so they could have a day of rest. One student raised her hand and told me this was impossible because she was 'committed to academic excellence'. Our society does force these kinds of questions on us. I doubt that Eric Liddell could win an Olympic gold medal today without training seven days a week. Our culture values success above all other things, but the price of success is high. So high, it seems, that it can lead us to disregard Scripture and go against common sense. Christians need to ask, 'Will I do what Scripture says or what my culture says?'

"God doesn't want believers gritting their teeth."

If this sounds too black-and-white to you, remember that this pattern of regular worship and rest is not a legal requirement. God doesn't want believers gritting their teeth, going to church and spending the rest of Sunday moping in their rooms. That misses the point, and will eventually bring frustration and failure.

The time of your life

The larger issue here is the sacredness of your time. Every moment of life is holy, set apart for God. Time is God's gift, given so his creatures may glorify him (*1 Corinthians 10:31*). Work, play and study can all be spiritual activities, given over to praising the Lord. When Christians commit themselves this way, their lives take on the quality of holiness.

Just as the workaholic shows by his life-style that he has consecrated himself to his job, and many physical fitness buffs adhere religiously

to their early morning run, Christians also show their commitments by the way they live.

One of the most beautiful and effective ways of consecrating ourselves is to establish a rhythm of worship in our lives. Many Christians practise a daily quiet time, even though the Bible never says, 'Thou shalt have Bible reading and prayer every morning for thirty minutes.' The quiet time is simply an effective, helpful way of committing oneself to God on a daily basis. If you have tried it, you know that it strengthens you and gives a sense of wholeness to your day.

If daily patterns of worship are good, why not have a weekly pattern too? The creation story shows God pausing to reflect at the end of each day's labours, but it also shows him taking

"The creation story shows God pausing to reflect."

a day of rest at the end of the week. Although the requirement of a Sabbath is no longer in place, this pattern of consecration is revealed by God's own actions. We have the privilege of mirroring the works of God by following his pattern.

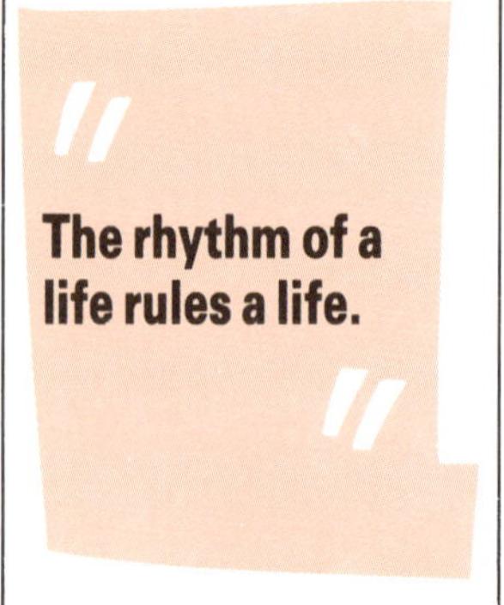

Perhaps this sounds a bit much to you. But all it means is giving a day for rest and worship every week, so that by your pattern of living you can show where your commitment lies. Consider this: the way a person spends his or her time influences his or her thinking as much as or more than anything else. The rhythm of a life rules a life.

Getting started

As I've wrestled with the significance of Sunday in my life, I've come up with a few suggestions that helped me steady my life rhythm. Maybe they'll help you too.

1. Be sure to attend your church's worship services. Hang around afterward and get to know the congregation. Your life will be enriched. Remember that church services are for worship. If you go only to get something out of the sermon, worship won't happen.

2. Relax and have fun. These are welcome parts of a day off. But you may want to avoid strenuous activities on Sunday. Why? Because the idea behind the day is to get both physical and spiritual rest. If Sunday is so tiring that Monday finds you useless, you've missed the point.

3. Sunday can also be a day for reaching into the lives of others. James defines true religion as that which visits 'orphans and widows in their distress' (1:27). Maybe you don't know anyone who is sick, lonely or in prison. But if you get involved in a local church for a while, you will meet them. And you can minister to them just by going to their house or hospital room for half an hour. This will enrich your life because those who give of themselves never fail to receive more than they give.

4. For those at school or college, perhaps the most effective thing you can do is to arrange not to study on Sunday – and not to work, if at all possible. That doesn't mean you need to take a blood oath never to study on Sunday again. It just means planning so that in normal circumstances you don't need to get the books out. It may mean studying on Saturday instead of putting everything off until Sunday.

I practised this habit while at Bible college. There were only two occasions in three years when I failed to keep it up – both times because of final exams which demanded extra attention. It feels fantastic to wake up Sunday morning and say, 'It's the Lord's Day – I don't have to study today!'

5. The Lord's Day should be a conscious attempt to practise the presence of God. Meditate on his presence of God. Mediate on his presence in your life, and pray that God will cause the richness of that presence to overflow into the other days of the week.

Sunday can be a day of light that illumines the entire week. It will be – if you give yourself wholeheartedly to its intended purposes.

Vance Hays

Practise the presence of God.

chapter seven

Finding gold on the silver screen

Ask any four people what they thought of the most recent film they saw, and you'll probably get predictable answers: 'I really liked the special effects.' 'The dancing was fantastic.' 'It was hilarious.' 'Great photography.' 'Too much sex.' 'Boring.' 'Extremely violent.' Short, easy critiques.

Our ability to be good film critics, to sift relevant themes and constructive ideas from what we watch, has been weakened by half-watching television, skimming popular magazines and half-listening to pop radio. We want to be entertained; we don't want to think. Let the critics be critical.

Becoming critical film buffs

But as Christians, we must be critical; everything we experience requires a Christian response. We can't drop off our faith back in our room and go unhindered into a darkened auditorium. If we casually stroll into *Room with*

a View or *The Mission*, Christ goes with us; if we blushingly tiptoe into *Swedish Nurses*, Jesus is there too. Whatever flashes across the screen must be seen through Christian eyes. What brings an audience to its feet might bring our Lord to tears.

Are films really worth that much effort, especially with everything else there is to do on offer?

It depends on the film. Some are poorly made or decidedly vulgar. Others have inconsequential stories with naive characters. But in the same way that incompetent authors shouldn't turn us away from literature or make us suspicious of Milton and Dostoyevsky, bad films should't make us shun all movies. There are some films we should walk out of. But others provide rich insight into our world and ourselves.

Despite peer pressure and your upbringing, it's up to you whether or not you're going to see a particular film. And it's relatively easy to know what to expect from a film before you buy your ice-cream and take your seat. Ratings and advertisements offer basic clues about what to expect, though ratings are never an accurate measure of quality. Assume that as you move from 'U' to '18' the frequency of nudity, violence and strong language increases. Even though some films earn a stronger rating based on only one word or scene, it's better to assume excess on the part of the film-makers; you'll save yourself the frustration of hating a movie you really shouldn't have seen in the first place.

Once you're seated in a dark cinema, you might gasp, 'But wait! I can't enjoy this. I have to be critical.' Don't worry. A critical, Christian approach to movies will help you clarify what's happening on the screen so that you can enjoy them even more.

Here are five categories to consider while the film is rolling.

Theme

No film is purely entertainment. Every film has

a point to make or a controlling, underlying theme.

The theme is usually a view of life that can be expressed in a sentence or two: mankind is headed for self-destruction (*Silkwood*); good can always out-manoeuvre evil (the James Bond films); every person has worth (*The Last Emperor*), or fantasy can come true (*Back to the Future*). Sometimes the theme is simple (*Fatal Attraction*). Other times it's complex. *Citizen Kane*, for example, has at least three themes: loving things more than people brings personal ruin; abandoning the joys of youth to achieve adult success ends in emptiness; and power corrupts. To determine a film's value, we must be able to discern its message.

Character

Characters must *do* something – reach a goal, effect change, learn some truth or teach a truth. Though a film may be technically proficient, something is wrong if the characters leave us cold.

Characters can't be much better than their dialogue. The words should reinforce the action and heighten the story. Are they realistic, expressing heartfelt emotions? Inane? With so much emphasis placed on big-screen visuals, don't underestimate dialogue – sight *and* sound, images *and* words, are ideally combined into a cohesive whole. And only film can capture this.

Don't forget to determine characters' moral inclinations. Characters' morality affects their perceptions and actions. In *Being There,* Peter Sellers' innocent and amoral Chance accepts and imitates everything he sees. Edmund Gwenn's moral Kris Kringle in *Miracle on 34th Street* wholeheartedly believes in fairy tales and wants to convince an unbelieving world. Vivien Leigh's Scarlett O'Hara, though not completely immoral, would stun the unflappable Kris Kringle with her pouting avarice. Each character is different; each provides a unique glimpse into the human soul and human behaviour.

"Each provides a unique glimpse into the human soul and human behaviour."

Plot

Ask: Is the story line entertaining enough to hold my interest? Believable? Old hat? Innovative? Intriguing? Does the producer seem to care about the viewer? A drama – or any film – without conflict lacks its most basic element. A horror film that exceeds our limits of belief leaves us tagging behind. The story should proceed logically within its own boundaries.

Tone

Tone creates the mood and is inseparably linked to theme, character and plot. Are the signals the film sends consistent? Are we increasingly drawn into the story? Are we enchanted – or manipulated? Or is the film

The good video guide

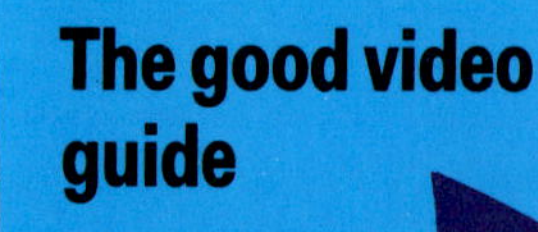

Ten videos worth watching. The list below is not an attempt to include everybody's favourites, but to select films which try to engage our minds as well as our emotions. Nine of the pictures have been on popular release at the cinema in recent years. Why not ask some friends round to watch and invite them to become film critics?

Ask some friends round . . .

The Mission (PG) – Warner Brothers Video

Spectacular epic set in South America where a Jesuit priest and a mercenary encounter the Guarani indians. The power of the sword against the power of love. An unusually sympathetic portrayal of missionaries which raises questions about pacifism or fighting for a just cause.

Amadeus (PG) – Thorn EMI Video

Peter Shaffer's version of history has court composer Salieri raging against God that he has given the gift of genius to a vain, giggling, childish Mozart. A powerful characterization of jealousy and a man who dares to challenge God.

simply visual and verbal assault, lacking tone altogether? If a film claims to be a comedy but doesn't make us laugh, something went wrong with its tone.

A film needn't be single-minded in tone, however. *Arsenic and Old Lace* and *Little Shop of Horrors* are good examples of films with two purposes – to make us jump and to make us laugh. They achieve a perfect balance between comedy and horror.

Offensive language, violence, nudity

Since the sixties, and the 'permissive revolution', censorship has increasingly been relaxed in Britain. What might once have got an 'X' certificate can now be seen with 'parental

The Deer Hunter (18) – Warner Home Video

Inadequate to call it a war film, the story traces the lives of a group of friends before and after service in Vietnam. A good choice to look at the justification of strong language and violent scenes in their context. The cost of war and friendship is brilliantly portrayed.

Cocoon (PG) – CBS/Fox

For those who prefer something lighter. This off-beat comedy stars geriatrics who find the secret of eternal youth by bathing in a pool visited by friendly aliens. The tongue-in-cheek humour hides real fears about old age, death and the afterlife. The ending poses us a choice.

Ghandi (PG) – CBS/Fox

Richard Attenborough's Oscar-winning film follows the charismatic leader's struggle to free India from the British Empire. Ghandi was the champion of non-violent resistance (like Martin Luther King). Watch out for him quoting Jesus to an English vicar.

continued . . .

The good video guide

Cry Freedom (PG) – to be released on video

Attenborough again, this time on apartheid in South Africa. A white journalist becomes involved with Steve Biko, a black rights leader. Through the newspaper man's eyes we are educated into the appalling facts of the South African situation. Based on true events which are still happening in that country.

Defence of the Realm (PG) – Rank Video

Political thriller that deserves to be seen. Should matters of national security be above moral question? Can the individual be sacrificed to the state? A frighteningly plausible version of the secret side of British government.

Falling in Love (PG) – CIC Video

Get out the tissues! One of a string of films taking up the story of an affair and marital break-up. This one deserves some credit for not over-romanticizing in realistic performances by Streep and De Niro. Ask yourself whether the film gives a balanced view of the two marriages involved.

The Killing Fields (15) – Thorn EMI Video

Superior war film based on true events in Cambodia as written by Dith Prahn (who appears as himself). An important portrayal of a merciless dictatorship. *The Killing Fields* also raises issues about the role of the press in wartime and the moral dilemmas facing a journalist.

Shadowlands (PG) – BBC Video

Award-winning television drama about C. S. Lewis's marriage to cancer victim Joy Davidman. Ultimate test of faith in the writer's life beautifully captures profound questions of suffering and a loving God.

Alan MacDonald

guidance' (which is often no obstacle).

So how do we avoid these situations? The most obvious solution is not to go to the pictures at all. For years conservative Christians considered this an accepted norm; today it is a legitimate response to the problem and should be considered.

But we must also be consistent. Books, TV, music and theatre are also media that can be misused. Yet, like those other media, films can enrich us if we select and view them intelligently and with discernment.

If we are confronted with offensive elements in the theatre, we should ask, What is the intent? Is the film just trying to shock? Titillate? Exploit? Or are the offensive items important to the story? In *The Deer Hunter*, the language may be offensive but it is arguably essential to the tension created. In *About Last Night*, though, the needless repetition of four-letter words is ridiculous. Likewise, *Rambo*'s violence exploits; *Platoon*'s violence is integral.

Well, what did you think?

As the curtain comes down and the lights come up we can add the finishing touches to our critique. Analysing a film with friends can be fun. Here are a few questions you can chat over in a group.

1. Did the plot move the action toward a worthy climax or did it drag on?

2. How were good and evil portrayed? How was God portrayed?

3. Were the characters real people or stereotypes? Did they show strengths missing in your own life – or were they prime examples of what not to be?

4. If the film contained questionable scenes, what was the intent? Did they arouse and exploit the audience, or were they an integral element of the story?

5. Which scenes were especially effective? Why?

If it was a good film, all of the elements should fit into place like pieces in a puzzle.

Hollywood is out to make money by entertaining us. But all those flesh-and-blood human beings who make up the film industry project their desires prejudices and values onto the screen. To write off such a dynamic combination as 'mere entertainment' is to miss its soul. Watching films critically can help you see anew the world that Christ died for. To let a film wash thrillingly over you and then allow it to evaporate as you step into daylight is to relinquish what films – both good and bad – are saying: I am a mirror of all the world.

Bob Bittner

"

See the world anew.

"

Reading between the lines

Why do we read books? C. S. Lewis says: 'Each of us by nature sees from one point of view with a perspective and a selectiveness peculiar to himself. . . . We want to see with other eyes, to imagine with other imaginations, to feel with other hearts, as well as with our own. . . . We demand windows.'

C. S. Lewis, *An Experiment in Criticism*, Cambridge University Press, 1965.

Reading gives us a window into someone else's world and we can see this world from the author's viewpoint. This is both exciting and dangerous, because if we enjoy the writing it is possible that we will subtly accept the writer's view of the world as true.

A world with a view

To read well, then, requires the ability to detect what a writer's worldview is and take a critical approach to it. As Christians our worldview is based on the Bible's teaching. But how that relates to the novel we are reading at the moment may not be obvious. Students of English literature are trained to read critically, but for those of us who read for pleasure it may help to know what to look for. 'All serious artists . . . are perfectly convinced of the truth as they see it,' wrote Joyce Carey. Behind their writing are certain assumptions about life. For example one writer may assume that God does not exist, that people are basically good and that society is always progressing. A different writer may assume God's existence, man's sinfulness and the decay of civilization.

Joyce Carey, *Art and Reality: Ways of the Creative Process*, Doubleday, 1961.

Happiness is a cigar

An example from advertising, where writing always has a declared interest, will illustrate. 'Happiness is a cigar called Hamlet.' If we break that down we can see the assumptions behind this slogan. 'Happiness' is *what we are all seeking and expect from life*. 'Happiness is . . .', *it exists and can be achieved if we know where to look*. 'Happiness is a cigar', *happiness has a form and a taste, it can be bought.* '. . . called Hamlet', *it also has a name, so don't settle for any imitations!*

Of course, reading between the lines of an advert is easier than doing the same with a book. Our sympathies for an argument or a character may easily cause us to miss the worldview that is assumed. Try to discover the hidden assumptions in a Jeffrey Archer novel. Or take Thomas Hardy's famous *Tess of the D'Urbevilles* in this extract:

'So the baby was carried in a small deal box . . . and buried by lantern-light, at the cost of a shilling and a pint of beer to the sexton, in that shabby corner of God's allotment where He lets the nettles grow, and where all the unbaptised infants, notorious drunkards, suicides, and others of the conjecturally damned are laid. Tess bravely made a little cross of two laths and a piece of string . . . putting at the foot also a bunch of the same flowers in a little jar of water to keep them alive. What matter was it that on the outside of the jar the eye of mere observation noted the words 'Keelwell's Marmalade'? The eye of maternal affection did not see them in its vision of higher things.'

Thomas Hardy, *Tess of the D'Urbevilles*, ch. 14, Penguin, 1978.

Our sympathies are obviously with Tess in her loss. The little ceremony shows her belief in 'higher things'. The tone of the author, however, betrays that *he* doesn't. God allows the nettles to grow, there is the doubt raised about damnation and finally the 'eye of mere observation' (the author's) sees a marmalade jar rather than higher things. Hardy doesn't state 'I don't believe in heaven', but the bitter tone betrays his worldview.

See the picture – read the book

How can we be aware of an author's worldview? Here are a few principles:

1. Do not attempt speed reading. Read for understanding.

2. Mark any key passages with a pencil. These

will help you find the main ideas of the book.

3. Note the tone the author is adopting (see above). Is he enthusiastic? Facetious? Detached? Does he engage your emotions and are they in conflict with your Christian beliefs?

4. What does the writer value most?

5. According to the writer/characters, what really exists?

6. What brings human fulfilment or happiness according to the author/characters?

Finally, why bother with all this? Isn't it better to read for escapism and entertainment? Learning to detect worldviews may seem like hard work at first, but you may soon find you can do it subconsciously and not worry about these steps. Then it can add an exciting dimension to your reading. It will help you focus on your own worldview and understand other people's. For Christians living in a godless society that is of vital importance.

Alan MacDonald

chapter eight

Tuning in: the truth about rock music

Mike grew up in a family that thought rock music was of the devil. Sometimes in school some of his friends would get together and go to hear a band in concert. They'd invite Mike. But the answer was always the same: No. He wasn't even allowed to have a radio in the house. Later, as he grew older and entered college, Mike was left to make those kinds of decisions on his own. Consequently, he listened to rock music constantly.

Once during his first year some friends invited him to go and hear a local band. After the first amateurish, deafening set, I asked him, 'What do you think?'

'Great,' he said. When the second show was over he said, 'Wow, that was great, too.'

'What are you saying?' I asked, shocked. 'This band is the worst.'

'Oh,' was all he said. He couldn't tell the difference; all he knew was that he liked rock music. No-one had ever taught him how to tell good music from bad music, which groups to listen to and which to stay away from. To him they were all the same.

All he knew was that he liked rock music.

Those who have flatly condemned rock music as weird, wanton and wrongheaded have nurtured thousands of Mikes – people who can't tell good rock from bad because they have no guidelines for judging it.

When you know what is good and how to recognize it, the choice is easy. However, when it comes to art (and when we talk about rock music we *are* talking about art), most people do not know what makes good art good, or how to recognize it.

Test 1: Is it good?

Like all art, rock does not come affixed with a sticky label which neatly lumps it into one of two categories: classic or rubbish. Art exists on a continuum from excellent to awful. In general, good music must possess the qualities we have come to expect of good art.

Below are some questions which you could use to evaluate any kind of art. Try answering some of them about the music you listen to:

- Is it novel and inventive? Is it one of a kind?
- Is it skilfully written and performed? (Whether a rock song or a symphony, the work should say, 'I was made by an expert.')
- Does it give you a glimpse into the mind of its creator? That is, rather than presenting a jumble of half-formed ideas, does this song reflect the artist's imaginative selecting, assembling and developing raw materials?
- Does it deliver all it promises? Is it complete and unified? (Good art must satisfy; there can be no loose ends or missing pieces.)
- Is it awkwardly patched together and forced-sounding, or does it seem to flow naturally, as if it had a life of its own apart from the artist?

Test 2: Is it true?

In his book *Art and the Bible* Francis Schaeffer describes four categories of art: bad art with a true message: good art with a true message; bad art with a false message; and good art with a false message. These are what I call the four arts, and they abound in rock music. Listen to any pop radio station: you will hear from ten to fifteen different songs in an hour, some bad, some good and each with a different message.

When good music's combined with a false message, we can get confused. Catchy music and clever lyrics give false messages a credibility they would not ordinarily have. By naturally responding to the song's quality, we may suspend judgment and accept its false message, too.

Rock stars don't try to trick us into believing lies; it just happens. As often as not, musicians are themselves ignorant of the truth and consequently in no position to communicate it to others. Many simply echo the myths of the modern world: 'Love's all you need,' 'You only live once; so live it up while you can', 'Happiness is all that matters,' and so on.

When it comes to communicating true messages, rock primarily falls short in the following areas:

Materialism Although many songwriters point out that wealth and material things can never ensure happiness, a good many more imply just the opposite. When Madonna bellows out that she's a material girl living in a material world, her tongue isn't completely in her cheek. Success is often presented stereotypically: obtaining more, getting your share, making your fortune, having it all.

Sex 'Love' usually means sex. Both men and women are presented as sexual objects existing solely to satisfy the desires of the other. Relationships in songs often focus on the sex act as the ultimate expression of love.

Hedonism Pursuing the 'good life' is part of the rock myth. Personal pleasure is life's highest aim. The Christian value of service is foreign to most popular songs.

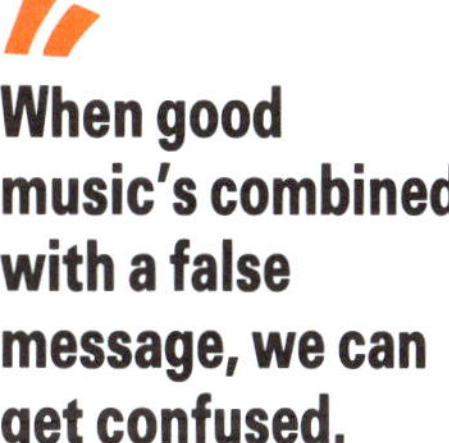

So, in the tangle of mixed messages presented by popular music, we have to decide what is true and what is false in a song, what to embrace and what to reject. If you're not used to paying close attention to what is being heard, you will have to make a conscious effort to discern a song's message as well as its emotional effect. Try asking these questions: Is this song's message consistent with the basic truths Christians

live by? What kind of feelings does this song evoke in me? Are these feelings healthy?

Deciding that a song has a true message does not mean deciding that we agree with what is being said or that it makes us feel good. A song may have a true message yet make us uncomfortable. For example, the message of the Geldof/Ure Band Aid anthem 'Do They Know It's Christmas?', that millions of the world's people are starving, does not make anyone feel good. Yet it's true. On the other hand, a Christian song implying that 'if you only trust Jesus he'll give you everything you want' might invoke good feelings, even though its message is false.

A song is not true just because it has the words *Jesus* or *God* in it. Neither is a song false because it omits those words.

... what kind of feelings?

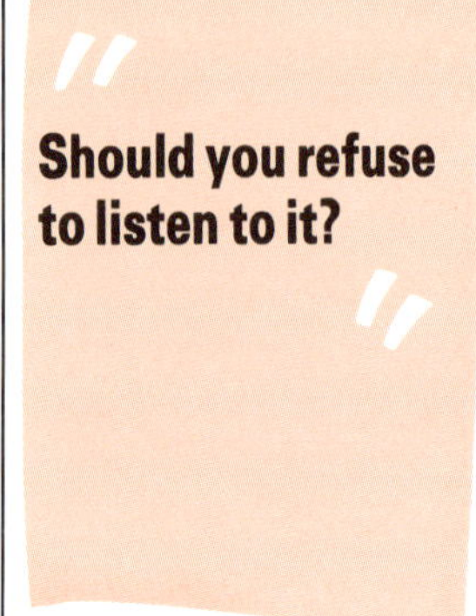

Making choices

If a song doesn't pass the tests of being good art and having a true message, should you refuse to listen to it? Though plenty of Christians are eager to dictate what we ought to listen to, only you can decide.

If, for example, a good song with a false message makes you doubt something you know to be right, then you should probably avoid it. But a word of warning: if we want the freedom to listen (or not to listen) to certain songs, then we must reserve judgment and allow others to make their own choices, too.

Rather than condemning rock, God's people should be in the position of encouraging whatever is good, worthy and true in popular music. And rather than blacklisting, condemning or otherwise writing off Christian rock bands who don't fit our stereotypes of what Christian musicians should be, we must encourage them to higher achievement. The Christian community and the world at large desperately need the creativity, enthusiasm, courage and vision Christian artists can bring.

Steve Lawhead

chapter nine

Translating your faith into social action

When I speak to Christians I see a lot of people who want, deep down inside, to be heroes, who long to change the world for God. But many get burned out because they don't feel one person can make a difference.

I want to make this as clear as I can: Jesus saved you so that he could work through you to accomplish things that he wants to have done in this world. Jesus saved you in order that you might be an agent for his revolution in the world.

I know that today's young Christians could change the world. But that's not going to happen. Why? Not because they're not committed to Christ, but because they don't see how they could effect change. Commitment without a methodology to carry it through is ineffective.

Whether you realize it or not, today you actually have more opportunities than ever before to get involved in social action of some kind – perhaps through a Christian organization or perhaps side by side with non-Christians through a secular charity. (If you're a student, you'll know that university and college campuses are a focal point for young, idealistic people to organize and try to effect change.)

Unfortunately, many Christian people feel too busy with college, work and church commitments to get involved in social action. Why should a keen Christian be concerned about social action, anyway? Aren't evangelism and Bible study more important?

I see a lot of people who want, deep down inside, to be heroes.

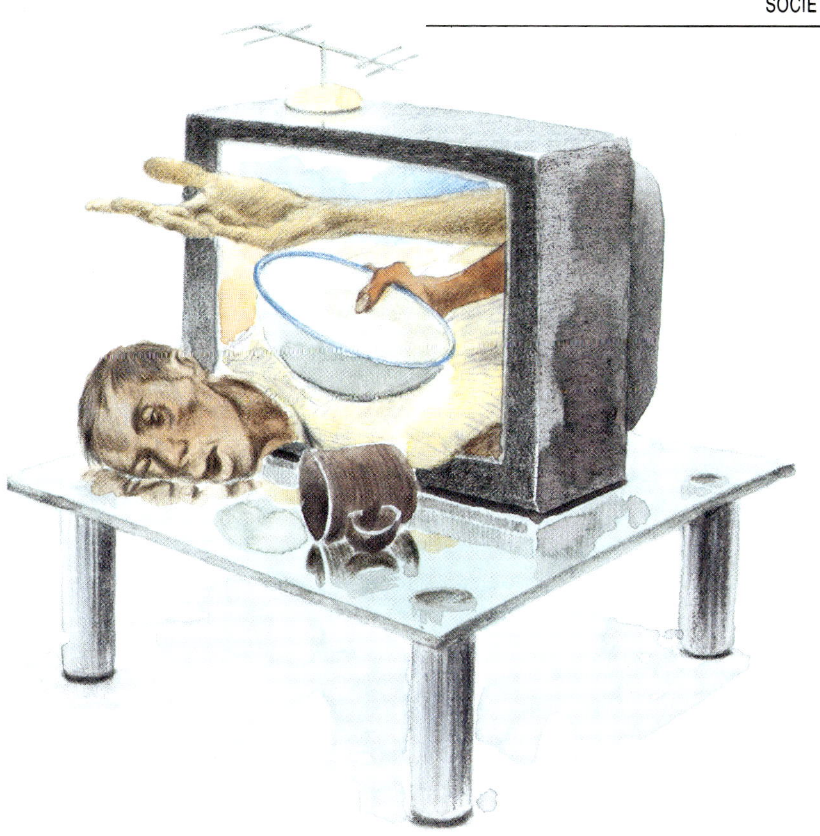

Jesus came to transform society

Jesus wasn't interested only in saving individuals so that they could go to heaven when they died. Jesus broke into history with a declaration that he had come to initiate the kingdom of God. Many of his parables were given to teach us some of the principles upon which this kingdom was to be developed. The Sermon on the Mount provided the ethic for this kingdom. When Jesus taught us how to pray he encouraged us to yearn that the kingdom might exist on earth as it already exists in heaven.

Jesus wants to create a revolutionary new society. Once we grasp that, we can begin to understand why he was crucified. The custodians of the status quo, who had a vested interest in maintaining the established social order with all of its oppression and injustice, predictably

To be a Christian is to have your heart broken by the things that break the heart of God.

opposed this man who called for the creation of a new regime. While his adversaries may have been blind to the fact that Jesus was the Son of God, they clearly recognized that he was socially dangerous. The accusations that they levelled at him as he moved toward the crucifixion expressed their fear of him. They said, 'He stirs up the people,' and that 'It is necessary for this man to die, that Israel (the established social order) might be saved.'

I am not attempting to reduce Christianity to some simplistic social gospel. God's kingdom does not become a reality simply by facilitating a few positive social changes with the expectation that all will be well if we can just eliminate corrupt institutional structures. On the contrary, there will be no kingdom unless it is populated by people who incarnate the nature and the values of the King.

People need to be saved from sin. They need to be made into new creatures before they can effect the institutional changes which are essential if the kingdom is to come 'on earth as it is in heaven'.

Jesus calls us to move beyond a desire for personal piety to a desire to serve others, especially those who are desperately poor. To be a Christian is to have your heart broken by the things that break the heart of God. To be a Christian is to be filled with righteous indignation over the fact that we affluent British live with a high level of indifference to the unjust privations of people around the world. The Jesus of Scripture beckons us to change a world in which 500 million people suffer from malnutrition while the rich in other nations suffer from overweight. He calls us to transform it into a world in which the needs of all people are satisfied.

I was once witn a voluntary work party who had just completed a month of exhausting labour rebuilding a Third World village which had been destroyed by a hurricane. On the day we were to leave the village the people threw a party for us. There was singing and dancing. Laughter abounded everywhere. As I stood at the edge of the party, looking on with pleasure and satisfaction, an old man of the village pulled me aside and said, 'You can tell me now. You're a communist, aren't you? You and your friends are communists. Right?'

I said, 'No, of course not. I oppose communism. I'm a Christian. What makes you think that I or my friends are communists?'

He said, 'You care about poor people.'

His response upset me more than I can say. Why aren't Christians known as the ones who are most concerned about the poor and the oppressed people of the world? Perhaps it's because we haven't been the most concerned.

Of course, God's kingdom is his to create; it will not be ushered in through our efforts. Actually, the kingdom of God will never become a complete social, historical reality until the Lord himself returns. But he continues to build it through us.

Feeling powerless?

But you say, 'What can *I* do? I mean, I'm just one young person struggling to get through history, let alone change the course of it. I feel powerless to change anything.'

In a sense, you're right. As an individual, you are relatively powerless. And the world believes that only the powerful can bring about social change. They think that the powerless count for nothing. But the Bible reminds us – through the lives of Jesus, John the Baptist, Mary, the prophets, the disciples and others – that it is through the powerless that the works of the powerful are brought to nothing.

In my own efforts to bring about social change, I have witnessed the effectiveness of powerlessness. A group of my students from Eastern College became very upset with one large corporation, Gulf and Western Industries, while we were doing missionary work in

A group got very upset with one large corporation . . .

the Dominican Republic. We became aware that this multinational corporation was taking land that should have been used to grow food for needy people in that poor country and using that land to grow sugar.

As you know, sugar is bad for you. So is coffee. So is tobacco. You may not know that if all of the land in the world that is presently being used to grow sugar, coffee and tobacco were used to grow food, we could cut malnutrition in the Third World by almost 50%.

Anyway, we were upset with Gulf and Western because we saw that they were growing sugar for people in the United States on land that we felt should have been used to grow food for needy Dominican peasants.

'You are God's stewards. He doesn't like the way you are running the company . . .'

One in a million

There were eleven of us, and each of us bought one share of stock in the company. I don't know how many millions of shares of stock there are in Gulf and Western, but we owned eleven of them. And you only need one share to go to the annual shareholders meeting. So each of us 'shareholders' went to the meeting and said our piece.

We were a bit arrogant about it, but we really laid into them: 'Hey! We don't like the way you are running this company! This company belongs to God.' In private confrontations following that meeting, we met with some of the company's top executives and told Jesus' story of a man who had a vineyard. The man went away on a long trip, but the people he left in charge of the vineyard didn't run it right. He sent messengers, but they wouldn't listen to the messengers. Then he sent his son, but the people put him to death. Jesus ends that parable with this question, 'What then should the owner of the vineyard do to the unfaithful stewards when he returns?'

We told all of that and more to these men. 'You are God's stewards. He doesn't like the way you are running the company, and so we have come as messengers. You had better listen to us, or God is going to come and get you.'

Looking back on our behaviour I have to admit we weren't Christlike or even fair. But what followed those encounters was incredible. We found out that the leaders of that company weren't bad men. In our talks with them they convinced us that they wanted Gulf and Western to be an instrument for good in the Dominican Republic.

About a year and a half after our discussions with Gulf and Western began I got a call from one of its executives. He said, 'Tomorrow we're going to have a press conference, and part of the reason we're holding it is to make an announcement about some of the issues we discussed with you. We want you to be among the first to know what's going to happen.'

And as I sat there dumbfounded, that executive told me that Gulf and Western was going to do the following. First, they would test the soil that made up their landholdings in the Dominican Republic, determine what land could be used to grow food, and shift that land from sugar to food production. Second, the company would make a commitment to build forty thousand new housing units for the sugar workers so that they would no longer have to live in the slums. Third, Gulf and Western would provide educational and health programmes, particularly in the eastern half of the country where their operations were located. The spokesman went on to say that his corporation had made a commitment of £50 million to be spent over the next five years in order to make all the promises a reality. Now *that*'s incredible.

"... now that's incredible ..."

Don't tell me today's young Christians can't effect change. We need to be willing to stand up and make things happen.

Ways you can make a difference

So how can you make a difference? Here are some ways you and your Christian friends can begin to bring peace and justice to your college, work place, community, country and world in the name of Jesus.

The first and best kind of social action is a Christian response to individuals in need: feeding the hungry, clothing the naked, healing the sick, and visiting those who are in prison. People have needs; Christians become aware of those needs; Christians do what Jesus would do – meet those needs.

"People have needs."

One warning: if you are not trying to share the love of Christ with those immediately around you, you have no legitimate right to move on to other types of social action. It is easy to become so concerned with the social injustices that are inherent in our political and economic systems that we pass over the suffering of people who confront us face to face in daily living. Jesus would remind us that if we cannot respond to those whom we can see, it is impossible to respond to a God whom we cannot see.

Adopt a grandparent. Phone an old people's home and find out at what times visitors are welcome. Then mingle and talk with some of the people there. Choose one or two elderly people to visit on a regular basis, to remember on special occasions, to take on short trips now and then – just to be a friend to. If you are doing this in a group, take time periodically to share joys, difficulties or concerns with each other and pray for your 'grandparents'.

Gifts for the needy. Usually the Salvation Army, WRVS or local Social Services Department will be aware of particularly needy families in your area. Find out their names, ages, clothing sizes and so on. Then get some friends together and pool some money you'd spend on yourselves to buy a gift for each member of the family or families you've chosen. The agencies will be able to advise on what is most needed and how it can be given.

Hospital visiting. Many patients get very few visitors. Get permission from a hospital administrator to visit some of these people on a regular basis. Nurses on duty can tell you which patients are most willing to have visitors, as well as the basics of hospital etiquette (don't lay down on the patient's bed to take a nap, *etc.*). Some hospitals have Sunday services you may be able to get involved with.

Holiday clubs. Young children and teenagers from poor areas and large housing estates are often bored during the holidays. Try getting together with the local church to organize a holiday club. You could run football or rounders matches, go to the cinema or organize other trips and events for kids whose lives are often dull and frustrating.

Day centre volunteers. Most areas have day centres or other institutions which care for those with learning difficulties (mentally handicapped). These places are often understaffed and grateful for volunteer helpers. There are many rewarding activities that can be done: perform music or drama with them, organize art and craft work, go on walks, accompany them to the shops, or even invite some to your fellowship or church meetings. As with any voluntary work, check with the professionals before you launch a project!

Prison ministry. One of the specific instructions Jesus gave the church was to minister to the needs of prisoners. There are many ways you can help: visit and become a prisoner's friend; write them letters; bring in a group to play a game against an institutional team; take a service for the prison chaplain; collect books for the library or buy something to make the institution more livable (such as a sound system or sports equipment).

Help to the Third World. Agencies such as World Vision and Tear Fund are involved in relief and development work in needy countries all

over the world. There are sometimes opportunities overseas for short- or long-term service, but there is always a need for donations. Money may go to providing urgent meals or medicines, agricultural development, or training nationals in practical skills.

Political action

This kind of social action should not be seen as a substitute for service projects that minister directly to the needs of hurting people. Your highest priority should be to minister to those who are suffering. But, in the long run, it does little good to minister to the victims of an evil system while doing nothing at all to change the system so that it produces fewer victims.

Ron Sider, a popular author and leader of Evangelicals for Social Action, tells the following parable:

A group of devout Christians once lived in a

Change the system so that it produces fewer victims.

small village at the foot of a mountain. A winding, slippery road with hairpin curves and steep precipices without guard rails wound its way up to one side of the mountain and down the other. There were frequent fatal accidents. Deeply saddened by the injured people who were pulled from the wrecked cars, the Christians decided to act. They pooled their resources and purchased an ambulance. Over the years they saved many lives, although some victims remained crippled for life.

Then one day a young man came to town. Puzzled, he asked why they did not close the road over the mountain and build a tunnel instead. Startled at first, the ambulance volunteers quickly pointed out that this approach (although technically quite possible) was not realistic or advisable. After all, the narrow mountain road had been there for a long time. Besides, the mayor would bitterly oppose the idea. (He owned a large restaurant and service station halfway up the mountain.)

The young man was shocked that the mayor's economic interests mattered more to these Christians than the many human casualties. Somewhat hesitantly, he suggested that perhaps the churches ought to speak to the mayor, an elder in the oldest church in town. Perhaps they should even elect a different mayor if he proved stubborn and unconcerned. Now the Christians were shocked. With rising indignation and righteous conviction they informed the young radical that the church dare not become involved in politics. The church is called to preach the gospel and give a cup of cold water. Its mission is not to dabble in worldly things like social and political structure.

Help the victims . . . or go for the structures?

Perplexed and bitter, the young man left. Is it really more spiritual, he wondered, to operate the ambulances which pick up the victims of destructive social structures than to try to change the structures themselves?

A change has got to come

Here are some ways you and your fellowship group can begin to change ungodly social structures:

Political canvassers. Contact the candidate of your choice and volunteer to work in the forthcoming campaign – delivering literature, making phone calls, making posters, whatever.

Letters to the editor. On crucial political issues, write letters to the editor of your local newspaper. These are usually published and read by hundreds, sometimes thousands of people – including candidates and policymakers.

Letter-writing campaigns. Never underestimate the impact of organizing a letter-writing campaign on an important issue. A hundred letters on a particular issue can easily sway the opinion of an MP who does not have strong convictions on a particular matter. (Every letter should address the issue and state whether you are for or against a particular piece of legislation, but each person who writes should do so individually.)

Pickets for Christ. Every political party has gatherings of some sort. If your party has ignored or taken what you understand to be an un-Christian position on a social issue of great concern, then picket that gathering. Get your group together, map out a strategy, spend a day making signs and banners, print up some press releases, and take a stand. You will probably get coverage on radio, television and the newspapers – giving you a chance to explain why your Christian commitment has led you to your position.

Tony Campolo

HELP WANTED: social action organizations who need you

Wondering what you can do to help serve others and effect godly change in society? Beside writing letters to your Members of Parliament you can contact a number of organizations. You will probably be aware of the large ones such as Oxfam, Amnesty International and UNICEF but here is a selection of some of the evangelical groups committed to social action:

Six of the best

CARE CAMPAIGNS

21a Down Street, London W1Y 7DN. 01-409-0111

Campaigning in local and national politics for law and public policy in harmony with Christian principles. Quarterly magazine: *Care News*.

CARE FORCE

130 City Road, London EC1V 2NJ. 01-250-1966

Sponsored by four evangelical societies, Care Force places young Christians in inner-city churches and caring organizations for a year's voluntary service.

PRISON FELLOWSHIP, England and Wales
PO Box 263, London SW1E 6HP. 01-582-6221
Christian support for prisoners and ex-prisoners, prayer/action groups for every penal establishment.

CHRISTIAN IMPACT
79 Maid Marian Way, Nottingham NG1 6AE. 0602 585731
Evangelical Christian society; co-ordinates research on contemporary social issues and appropriate Christian response; publications, study groups, action.

TEAR FUND
100 Church Road, Teddington, Middlesex TW11 8QE. 01-977-9144
Working with Christians around the world to combat poverty and injustice; a wide range of educational and promotional material is available, as well as ways to relieve poverty.

WORLD VISION OF BRITAIN
Dychurch House, 8 Abington Street, Northampton, Northants., NN1 2AJ. 0604–22964
International, interdenominational, Christian humanitarian agency involved in relief and development work in the Third World.

Frameworks for living series

'Direct access to live issues'

David Porter

USER'S GUIDE TO THE MEDIA

How to enjoy and evaluate soaps, adverts, news, the message.

- Don't scrub soap
- What a friend we have in Volkswagon
- I photograph best from the left
- More is said than what is spoken

Joyce Huggett

LIFE IN A SEX-MAD SOCIETY

Handling intimacy, sex and friendship.

- The petting problem
- Cooling the sex urge
- Is sexual sin unforgivable?
- The pain of splitting up

J. John

DEAD SURE? about yourself, life, faith.

A credible explanation of Christianity for today.

- Modern problems
- Anxiety, stress, loneliness
- The Jesus story in modern English
- No resurrection – No Christianity
- Why believe?

Alan MacDonald with Tony Campolo, Val Howard and others

THE TIME OF YOUR LIFE

- Getting more from pop and film
- Enjoying sport and friends
- Social times and social action
- The place of drink and parties

Frameworks for living series

Colourful and readable.
Straight to the heart
of today's big issues.

Also released:
Life in a sex-mad society
by Joyce Huggett

When you're a single person what can you do about your desire for intimacy, embracing . . .'

'We're very much in love. We're sorely tempted to go too far too soon physically. . .'

The petting problem – cooling the sex urge – Is sexual sin unforgivable? – The pain of splitting up – and much more.

Direct and wise advice on handling sex and friendship from the internationally respected counsellor Joyce Huggett.